Songbirds of Europe

HENK VAN DEN BRINK

 **REBO**
PRODUCTIONS

© 1996 Zuid Boekproducties, Lisse
© 1997 Rebo Productions Ltd
text: Henk van den Brink
cover design and layout: Ton Wienbelt, The Hague
picture editing: Marieke Uiterwijk, TextCase
editing and production: TextCase, Groningen
typesetting: Hof&Land Typografie, Maarssen
translation: Euro Business Translations, Bilthoven

ISBN: 1 901094 53 7

Contents

Foreword

Songbirds are the ideal subject for the beginning bird-watcher to study. You can find them everywhere, and you don't have to go far to see them. In fact, when it's so cold outside that your face turns numb you can sit cosily by the fire and watch through the window as the tits, finches and thrushes come down for peanuts, seed cakes and fruit.

You can learn a very great deal about the behaviour of birds from this comfortable vantage point. A certain amount of background knowledge can help you to understand this behaviour and put it in context, and I hope that this book will contribute to your enjoyment.

Watching songbirds can also be a pretty frustrating pastime, particularly when the birds keep darting off into the bushes or behind tree trunks and branches just as you've got them focused in your bin-oculars. This is yet another reason for learning to identify the sounds that they produce, particularly the sound at which songbirds excel, the song. A whole new world opens up to people who can recognize birds from their song. And if you go out bird-watching armed with this knowledge your enjoyment will be doubled.

One cannot help but admire songbirds. Take the wren. This tiny bird can produce an amazingly loud noise. As you will learn, the musical talents of birds derive from very basic –not to say mundane– motives.

But of course this is just part of the story. Because it remains astonishing that these underlying motives have led to such a rich, musical language which we can always enjoy.

Henk van den Brink

Female house sparrow

Introduction

The great majority of birds that live in our environment are songbirds. Where I live, for example, I could stay indoors all year round and still always be able to see or hear songbirds.

On a spring morning I simply have to open the window to hear the blackbird, the great tit, the wren, the robin and the lesser whitethroat singing in the garden, and sometimes even a skylark soaring over the meadows in the distance.

In the winter I only have to look out of the window to see blackbirds enjoying the pieces of apple and bread I have put out for them, to see the robins and wrens busily searching for anything edible, to see the great tits and blue tits pecking at the peanut feeder and, occasionally, to spot a goldcrest in the conifers.

The robin has no fear of man

The desert whitethroat does not really belong in Europe. Its breeding grounds are in Africa (the Sahara) and Asia. This individual is well off course in the Dutch coastal resort of Scheveningen, where it attracted a great deal of attention.

The shrikes (this is a great grey shrike) are an unusual family of songbirds. With their curved bills they look like miniature birds of prey, and they behave like them too. They catch mice, voles like this one, frogs, lizards and even small songbirds. The great grey shrike can hover like a kestrel when hunting for prey.

It is not easy to find a place where there are no songbirds at all. Perhaps in parts of major cities, but even there a roofing tile suitable for nesting and a little patch of greenery –a single shrub or tree, for instance– are enough for, say, a house sparrow and a blackbird.

A great many songbirds are happy around people. They have adapted to the environment created by man and take advantage of the opportunities it offers: gardens where all sorts of trees and shrubs grow, where nest boxes have been put up and there is food on bird tables in the winter.

Songbirds are often colourful birds who enjoy the limelight. And they make our existence that much more pleasurable with their song. It is with good reason that they are so popular with us humans. This popularity sadly has its downside too.

If the birds do not seek out the company of humans of their own accord, they are sometimes brought there against their will. Down through the centuries songbirds have been kept in cages and aviaries to sit permanently looking beautiful and delighting the owner with their song.

What are songbirds?

Not all birds that sing are songbirds. The 'booming' of the bittern, the snipe's 'chick-a-chick', woodpeckers drumming, the nocturnal hooting of the tawny owl and the call of the cuckoo could all be described as forms of song. If song were to be the criterion, we would have to call almost all birds songbirds, which would not make a great deal of sense.

On the other hand, there are birds which do not produce a sound that we would describe as song and which are nonetheless 'officially' classified as songbirds. To explain this seeming paradox, we need to know a little bit about scientific system. To bring order to the apparent chaos, biologists have divided all forms of life into groups according to their relationships. The animal kingdom is divided first into classes –the birds are one, the others include fishes and mammals.

The classes are split into orders, the orders in their turn into families, families into genera, and finally genera into species. The songbirds or Passeriformes are an order. The groups are distinguished primarily according to anatomical characteristics. The most important common features of songbirds are the structure of the vocal organ (the 'syrinx', the avian equivalent of the larynx) and of the toes, which are shaped so that they can easily grasp branches.

The fieldfare is a winter visitor in large parts of Europe. It breeds in Scandinavia and Eastern Europe

These anatomical characteristics tell us a great deal about songbirds' lifestyles. Most species live in a habitat where there are trees and bushes. They are generally small birds, lack of size being a precondition for moving easily among the leaves and branches.

Most songbirds devote a great deal of effort to their song: they have quite extensive, sometimes very varied and, to our ears, extremely melodious songs in their repertoires. Again, this is closely related to their habitat: colour or movement will not help you to stand out in woods or in bushes –sound will.

We cannot, however, use these aspects of their lifestyles as characteristics by which we can identify songbirds. They are 'rules' with a great many exceptions. We find songbirds in the open fields – the skylark is a classic example. There are even songbirds that live high up in the mountains, as we will see in chapter 4.

And there is a family of songbirds whose members are not only all fairly hefty, they are none of them exactly renowned for the beauty of their song: the Corvids or crows. In the official classification, however, crows are songbirds. At 65 cm from the tip of its beak to the end of its tail, the raven is the largest songbird in Europe. This is a bird that is never likely to qualify as a songster in anyone's book!

And yet some members of the crow family can produce more than a raucous 'caw' – they can in fact sing quite well. The jay, for example, is a very accomplished singer, although its song is infrequently heard and it sings softly and hesitantly, as if rather ashamed of it. Jackdaws cannot really sing, but they do make dozens of different sounds, all of which mean something specific.

The Belgian artist Achilles Cools spent years studying the social life of the jackdaw and the

The wren can be found in gardens all year round, foraging for food under bushes and shrubs

Goldcrests sometimes appear in gardens during the migration period, particularly if there are conifers

Left: In some years you will not find a rose-coloured starling anywhere in Europe. In other years, however, huge flocks of them appear in Southeastern Europe, where they breed in great colonies. After a very short breeding season they rapidly return to Asia. This pattern is linked to the behaviour of grasshoppers, the birds' principal source of food

Following pages:
Male house sparrow. House sparrows are to be found wherever there are people. You will not find them in unpopulated areas. The bond is so strong that you have to wonder where house sparrows lived before there were any people

Great tits are true 'followers of civilization' and are often found in the vicinity of people. This great tit has interpreted the concept of a 'nest box' very broadly indeed

part played by 'jackdaw language'. He wrote about it in the book 'Jackdaws in the Mirror'.

Songbirds are by far the largest order of birds. Almost half of the approximately 9000 species in the world belong to this order. Of the 400 or so species of birds that breed in Europe, half are songbirds.

In terms of numbers of individuals, the predominance of the songbirds is significantly greater. Most songbirds are small, and as a rule small species of animals are much more numerous than large ones. There are tens of millions of common songbirds like robins, blackcaps and finches in Europe. They are common in every country, and in virtually every region.

So it is not difficult to find a great many songbirds close to home. Obviously it will be easier if you live in the country or in a leafy suburb, but a city-dweller who keeps his eyes open will have no trouble spotting ten or more species during a walk in the local park. And if you can recognize birds by their song, you will be able

A spotted flycatcher feeds the young while the other parent looks on

Below and below right: some species also have a number of sub-species. One of the best known is the yellow wagtail
From left to right: the British sub-species, with a yellow head, the Central European 'nominate' form, with grey-blue and white markings on the head, and the Balkan yellow wagtail with a completely black cap

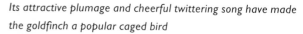

Its attractive plumage and cheerful twittering song have made the goldfinch a popular caged bird

to identify thirty or forty species in May and June, when all the migratory birds have returned.

As well as these widespread species, there are also songbirds that only occur in the far-flung corners of Europe. You will search in vain for the black wheatear anywhere outside Spain; and the trumpeter finch can only be found at the southernmost tip of Spain.

The range of Rüppell's warbler does not extend beyond Greece. The songbird with the smallest range is the Corsican nuthatch. It is found only on Corsica (making it an 'endemic' island species, the only one in Europe!) and it never leaves the island.

The rose-coloured starling appears in Europe in some years and not in others. It is an Asian songbird, which in pursuit of its food –grasshoppers and crickets– sometimes arrives in great flocks in the Balkans and breeds there. In other years you can look in vain for a single rose-coloured starling.

And finally there are the visitors: these are species that are not indigenous to Europe, but have landed here by accident because they have flown too far west from Asia during their migration, have been blown across the ocean

Songbirds are designed to manoeuvre through dense vegetation, as this whitethroat demonstrates. The toes curl easily around twigs and stems

Members of the crow family, like the jackdaw, are classified as songbirds. Jackdaws cannot really sing, but they make dozens of different noises, all of which have a specific meaning

Belgian artist Achilles Cools spent years studying the social life of jackdaws and the part played by 'jackdaw language'. He wrote about it in his book 'Jackdaws in the Mirror'

from America by west winds or have been carried out of Africa by strong southerlies.

What is birdsong?

While birdsong may not be the sole prerogative of songbirds, it is, however, very much their domain. They did not, after all, get their name for nothing. The nightingale enjoys the greatest fame when it comes to musical versatility, but there are in fact songbirds with an even more extensive repertoire.

This is why I devote a great deal of attention in this book to the phenomenon of birdsong. When we think about birdsong we are immediately confronted with two questions:

what is birdsong and what distinguishes the song from other sounds made by birds?

Birds make all sorts of sounds. Almost all species have a repertoire of a number of sounds, ranging from just a few to dozens of different ones; most of which are short, simple calls which are clearly linked to a specific situation. They can be heard, for instance, when the bird takes flight or when it lands, when it is alone or in a flock.

These sounds almost always have a clearly defined function. They are used, for example, to establish contact with other members of the same species, 'here I am', to warn the young of trouble, to draw the attention of others in a flock to impending danger, to beg for food (the 'begging' cries of young birds in the nest). True song is generally longer and more complex than all these sounds or 'calls' and consists of a greater variety of notes.

However, it is impossible to draw a sharp line. In the case of the musical song of the blackbird, no one would doubt that this is song in the true meaning of the word. But certain types of cheeping by house sparrows are also forms of song, even though we do not recognize them as such.

Important differences also lie in the situation, the context, in which the song is heard. While most sounds are related to specific situations, song appears to burst forth spontaneously at any moment.

The song is also repeated for longer – from a few minutes to several hours. And finally –although there are some exceptions– song is usually produced by males. This all has to do with the functions of song, which I shall discuss in chapter 1.

You will find chaffinches everywhere. There are millions of them in Europe

The songbird with the smallest range of all is the Corsican nuthatch. It occurs only on Corsica (which makes it an 'endemic' island species - the only one in Europe) and never leaves the island

CHAPTER I

Why do birds sing?

Song has two main functions: to mark
out a bird's own area (its territory) and
to attract a female.
Experiments have clearly demonstrated
the essential function of song in establishing territory and in mating.

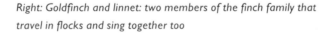

*Right: Goldfinch and linnet: two members of the finch family that
travel in flocks and sing together too*

*The rock thrush -this photograph is of the colourful male- nests
in the Alps and in mountainous areas in Southern Europe. The
echo effect of the rock face gives its melodious song a special
panache*

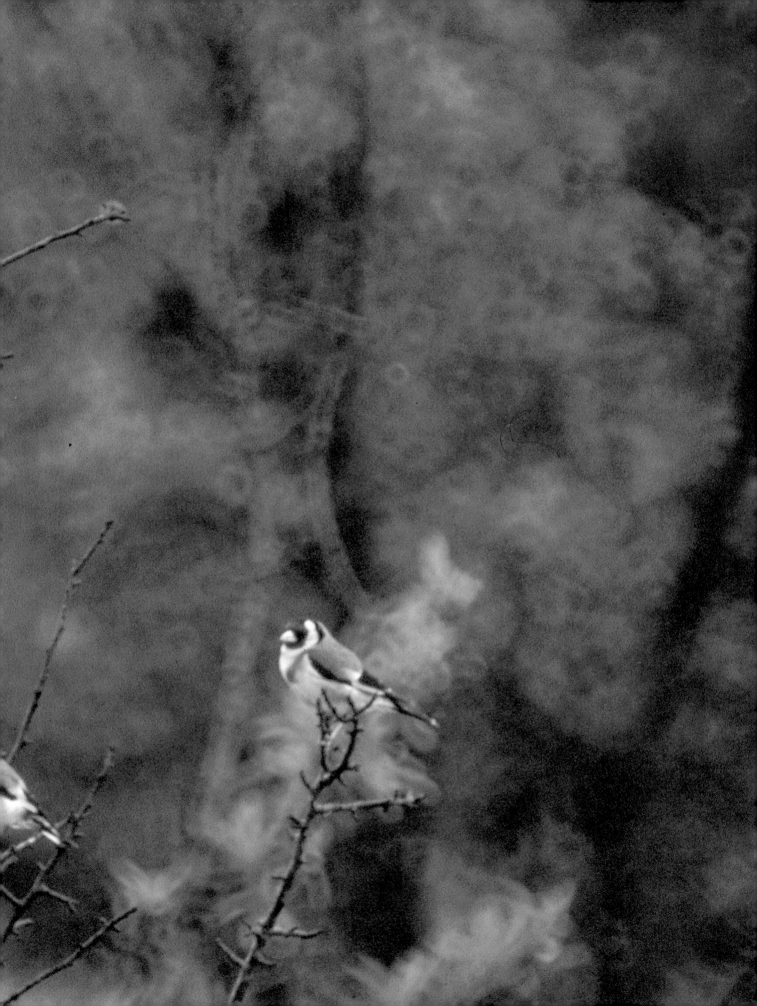

In many birds, the male is more colourful than the female. Songbirds are no exception. This female bullfinch (right) is very attractive, but she can't hold a candle to the male (left) with his magnificent rose-red breast

Right: All the effort this reed warbler has put into finding a territory and a mate, and building a nest, is simply serving to ensure the continued existence of another species. The nest contains a lusty young cuckoo, who has long since heaved the baby warblers overboard

Establishing a territory

An inconspicuous mountain-dweller: the rock sparrow, which looks not unlike a female house sparrow

As everyone knows, you can hear far more birdsong in the spring than at any other time of the year. But the birds are not singing for joy at the coming of spring or the fine weather. There is an unquestionable link between their singing and the breeding season; what's more in ninety-nine percent of cases it is the males that are singing. By singing, a male establishes the existence and boundaries of his own territory and attracts a female.

Experiments have clearly demonstrated the essential function of song in establishing territory and in mating. A singing bird is proclaiming his territorial rights and singing as long and as beautifully as he can to make an impression on a potential partner.

However, there are exceptions to every rule; some birds sing the whole year round, there are

species in which the females also sing and there are other, sometimes surprising and largely unexplained situations in which birdsong can be heard.

In many species of birds, the males return to the breeding site earlier than the females, and they generally start to sing almost immediately. If you take the time to watch a singing male and see what he does, you will soon realise that he remains within a particular area which he appears to be marking out with his song. When the neighbour starts to sing, he will respond to the challenge right away. If he succeeds in attracting a female, the pair will remain in this territory for the rest of the breeding season. The nest will be built there too.

Birds that belong to a different species, can enter the territory unhindered; the invisible borders do not exist for them. But males of the same species who stray into the area will be set upon immediately. A brief chase is usually enough to see off the intruder – a stranger or a

The paddyfield warbler is found in reedbeds on the north coast of the Black Sea. Distinguishing it from the reed warbler by appearance is a job for experts. The song is the best guide

Greenfinches adore rose hips. The male is on the left and the female on the right

neighbour with territorial ambitions. Sometimes it can develop into an actual fight, with the birds rolling over one another and the feathers flying. Very occasionally, one of the

warring parties may even sustain an injury. And yet the males do not spend their time constantly squabbling over boundaries. They cannot afford to, because they have far too many other things to do. Song plays an important role in preventing arguments. Song acts as a proclamation of the bird's species and at the same time as a

Sand martins return from tropical Africa in spring. Since they nest in colonies, they do not engage in territorial behaviour

Once the territory boundaries have been established and the birds have paired up, it is time to start building the nest. A female linnet with nesting material

Rüppell's warbler breeds only in the southeastern corner of Europe, in Greece and Turkey

Previous pages: There is occasionally time for a bath, as these linnets demonstrate

warning: this is my territory, keep out. The fact that one function of song is to make many fights unnecessary has been conclusively demonstrated in experiments. Male songbirds were caught, temporarily deprived of their ability to sing (by means of a minor operation on their vocal chords which did no lasting damage) and returned to their own territories. These males had the greatest difficulty in defending their territories. They constantly had to fight off intruders, were often forced to yield parts of their territory and sometimes even had to give it up altogether. In another experiment male great tits were captured. Some of them were then replaced with loudspeakers playing great tit song while others were not. The empty spots without loudspeakers were quickly taken over by other males; the sites with a loudspeaker remained unoccupied for a very long time.

In addition to song, visual signals and arresting behaviour help in marking out the territory. For songbirds that live in woods and bushes, the role of these signals and this behaviour is limited. They are only any use when a rival is close by. Then the feathers are fluffed up, the head is raised in the air and the wings are spread.

The purpose of the robin's orange breast feathers is easy to understand if you ever manage to see a robin fighting its own reflection in a mirror.

If you want to see the black wheatear you will have to go to the extreme southwest of Europe, to Spain

Following page: male great grey shrike on the look-out

The male robin recognizes this as a rival and attacks the enemy. I have seen a robin persistently flying and pecking at a car wing mirror. For birds that live in open fields, visible characteristics and behaviour are very important in demarcating their territory. In the spring ruffs have a large, strikingly coloured ruff which they raise during their mock battles on their display arenas. Even more spectacular is the courtship display of the great bustard, which turns its tail and wings inside out, transforming itself in an instant from a dullish brown bird to a ball of dazzling white feathers. Many of the stilts perform remarkable aerobatics in their

Male great tits that can no longer sing have to fight constantly with other males to keep their territories.
They often end up losing their patch. Song is a means of asserting your property rights

For birds that live in the open, outward display is often a very important part of the courtship process. These ruffs are having a ritual fight with erect ruffs

More outward display: the courtship ritual of the great crested grebe

The bluethroat has plenty of attributes to attract attention. The male sings beautifully and has a magnificent blue breast

Both males and females can also use the red panels at the base of the tail as a signal

Female wheatear. The white rump is a striking signal for the field-dwelling wheatear, particularly in flight

courtship displays, tumbling through the air with unusually slow or fast wing-beats to reveal striking coloured patterns on tail and wings. In almost all cases, this visual display is accompanied by arresting sounds.

By establishing territories, the birds are distributed more or less evenly in an area during the breeding season. In other words, territory demarcation prevents overpopulation in a particular area. For most songbirds this is vital, because they have to be able to find enough food for themselves and their young within a relatively small radius around the nest.

The size of the territories depends on the

Although this grasshopper warbler did his very best, his efforts came to nothing. This male turned up in Holland -far to the west of the normal breeding area- so his chances of attracting a female were slim. After performing day and night for some time, to the delight of the bird watchers who had flocked to see him, one day the bird simply vanished. Nevertheless this was a forerunner of future nesting. The grasshopper warbler is moving slowly but surely westward

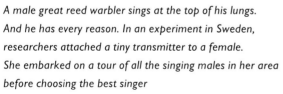

A male great reed warbler sings at the top of his lungs. And he has every reason. In an experiment in Sweden, researchers attached a tiny transmitter to a female. She embarked on a tour of all the singing males in her area before choosing the best singer

amount of food available. If food is plentiful, each family needs only a small space, so territories are small and density is high. Conversely, where food is scarce, territories are larger and the density is lower.

Finding a partner

If a bird carries on singing day in and day out, while other members of the same species have gone quiet, you can be virtually certain that it is

A female stonechat (right) would be wise to choose an actively singing male (left). Males that sing a lot usually do more to help in guarding the nest and feeding the young

a male who has not found a mate. This is a clue to the other main function of song: finding a partner.

Tirelessly singing males like this may sometimes be birds that have fetched up outside their normal breeding area. In this case, their chances of finding a mate are small. Nevertheless they do occasionally succeed, and if the pair then breeds successfully, a bridgehead is established to extend the breeding area. The singing males of the red-breasted flycatcher, northern nightingale and grasshopper warbler that occasionally turn up as far north and west as Holland may be the heralds of colonization in the future.

Left: Male great reed warbler

Experiments with birds in captivity have shown that females are undoubtedly attracted by the song of males of the same species. Playing a tape recording of the song of males actually proved to be enough to stimulate females into spontaneous courtship behaviour. Proof that females choose their partners on the basis of the quality of their song came from research done on great reed warblers in Sweden. The researchers fitted several female great reed warblers with tiny transmitters so that they could be tracked in the field wherever they went.

The researchers had also mapped all the territories of the males. The females followed a route through the site (a reedbed) that took them to all the territories at least once, before

Female chaffinch. Females kept in captivity can be sexually stimulated by playing them recordings of the right song

finally making their choice between one and three days later.

The qualities females look out for above all are the duration of the song (both the length of the song itself and the number of times it is sung) and the variety, or in other words the size of the repertoire.

The female great reed warblers in the Swedish study all chose males who sang long songs. A preference for an extensive repertoire of songs

Left: A sedge warbler in full song. Female sedge warblers go for the males with the biggest repertoire of songs

has also been found in the related reed warbler and in other species.

This raises the question of whether males who sing for longer and more melodiously really are better males – better husbands, better fathers. It is likely that males who sing most often and longest have the best territories. They can spend a lot of time singing, so they evidently do not have any difficulty in finding enough to eat. Whether the duration of the song also really tells us anything about the qualities of the male himself is less clear.

One thing is, after all, closely related to the

the order of the day. Males and females are as bad as each other. The dunnock, an unobtrusive and apparently modest little bird that frequently nests in parks and gardens, often runs a ménage à trois – a male with two females

It is not until after sunrise, when the earliest birds have already fallen silent again, that the simple, unassuming song of the pied flycatcher is heard

Dunnocks are not as prim and proper as they look. Threesomes - one male and two females or one female and two males- are not uncommon. Males and females have conflicting interests: the male wants to produce as many offspring as possible, while the female wants to keep two or even three males in tow so that they can all help in feeding the young

other: males with large territories have probably been the earliest to arrive at the nesting site or are the most capable of defending their territory, or both. They are therefore probably the strongest and fittest males. Studies have found that male stonechats who sing more are also more help in defending the nest and feeding the young. A large song repertoire with a lot of different melodies probably indicates a male who is a real tough nut.

Incitement to adultery

The song activity decreases in the course of the breeding season. There is no longer any need to sing: the boundaries of the territory have been established and the pairs have been formed. Nevertheless, most males do not become completely silent. A late intruder can be a reason to start up again. The song may also help to strengthen or confirm the bond between the pair. And then there is another aspect. In the past, it was generally thought that birds led an exemplary family life. More recently, however, it has become increasingly clear that adultery is

Starlings like to sing in company; in this case there are only two of them, but you will often see larger groups

The redpoll is a member of the finch family that lives mainly on birch seeds. Redpolls congregate in flocks during the winter, and sometimes sing in chorus

or a female with two males. Male and female have conflicting interests: the male wants to produce as many progeny as possible, while the female would rather have two or even three males in tow to help in feeding the young. It appears that song is a weapon that males use to serve their own ends: it keeps potential competitors away and can at the same time entice neighbouring females to commit adultery.

Song at other times

Not all birdsong can be explained in terms of the functions of territory demarcation and mating. There are birds, for instance, which you can hear singing all year round although not as frequently as in the spring. In a species like the robin this is easily explained, since robins defend feeding territories in the autumn and winter. It therefore makes sense for female robins to sing too during this period. But there

are several species which sing at times other than the breeding season, without any obvious reason.

And in other species, too, the females sing occasionally, usually shorter and less complex songs than the males. These songs may have a function that we do not yet understand. Perhaps it is simply a physical question, a reaction to the weather or to the length of the day, which affects the hormone balance and stimulates the bird to sing. Or could it be that birds actually do sing just because they feel good?

Choruses of birdsong at other times of the year also appear to be an expression of contentment. This is a phenomenon for which no acceptable explanation has yet been found.

Starlings and sparrows love to get together for a

Following pages: Redwings are winter visitors from the conifer forests of the north. Outside the breeding season they live in flocks. They give delightful performances of choral singing when they migrate

With its enormous bill the hawfinch is a striking sight. However, you will find them hard to spot during the breeding season because they lead an inconspicuous existence high in the tree-tops. If you want to know where hawfinches are to be found and how many there are, you will have to learn to recognize their song

chat. Siskins sing in chorus while stripping the alders in flocks. Other members of the finch family, like the linnet and the redpoll, regularly sing in chorus. In spring and autumn, you can come across flocks of redwings on their way from their breeding grounds to their winter quarters or vice versa, all sitting together singing in the treetops.

Whether or not birds sing out of contentment is open to question; in any event they do sometimes sing at the other extreme – when their lives are in jeopardy. Great tits and blue tits often burst into song when they are in danger of being caught by a sparrowhawk. The alarm call of a wren can also suddenly turn into song. 'Nervously' twittering swallows often signify a sparrowhawk or hobby in the vicinity. According to one theory, birds sing in these situations to demonstrate their strength: I'm strong and I'm not afraid! You won't get me! There sometimes also seems to be a sort of song of triumph by birds that sing loudly as soon as the danger is past. In these cases, the song may be a way of relieving fear and stress.

Counting breeding pairs by listening

When you walk through the woods, you will see only a fraction of the birds that are actually there. But you can certainly hear them! If you can recognize the species by their song, you can work out with a fair degree of accuracy which species are in the wood in spring. What's more, the song will tell you roughly how many breeding pairs of each species there are. After all, each singing bird represents a territory, and almost every territory indicates a breeding pair. This fact is the basis of a method that birders use to record the breeding bird population in areas with dense vegetation like woods and marshes. The researcher criss-crosses his area several times during the breeding season, carrying with him a detailed map on which he marks all the singing birds. At the end of the season he essentially superimposes these maps, and this gives him a picture of the sites of the territories. The number of territories is obviously not exactly the same as the actual number of breeding pairs.

There will not necessarily have been a female in every territory. The only way to establish the precise number of breeding pairs is to look for all the nests. But to do this you would have to comb through every bush and climb every tree. This would take far too much time and cause a great deal of disturbance. And even then, how could you possibly say for certain that you had found every single nest? Anyway, the count does not have to be as exact as all that. What really matters is the reason for the study.

If you want to compare the bird population in one area with that in other areas, you must count in exactly the same way in all the different areas. If you want to know whether the number of birds is increasing or declining, you must make sure that you use precisely the same method for your count every year.

The hobby, in this case a female, preys on songbirds

How do birds sing?

Birdsong is infinitely varied: differences in duration, different timbres, different themes and variations, warbles, whistles, rattles, trills and many, many more sounds for which words fail us. Some birds have extremely simple songs. The chiffchaff simply repeats its own name over and over again; the spotted fly-catcher's song is essentially the same as the sounds it produces the rest of the time, but slightly louder and faster. In contrast, we have the song of the nightingale, a concerto that puts human composers in the shade. Some species are able to use the sounds they can produce to keep on creating new songs –songs that can sometimes last for minutes at a time. The marsh warbler can mimic the calls of dozens of other species. Why some birds sing simple songs and others highly complex ones is a riddle that has yet to be solved.

As well as variation between species, there are also differences within a single species. Birds are not born knowing their songs, they have to learn them. And it takes them remarkably little time to do. This means that they are able to listen well and have a very good musical memory.

From the shelter of the green beech leaves the wood warbler sings his song; it has two distinct parts – a dry, ticking rattle and a melancholy whistle

In Europe, trumpeter finches (female on the left, male on the right) only occur in the southernmost part of Spain. They produce a sound very like the horn of a toy car

Forms of birdsong

A striking feature of a great deal of birdsong is its 'pure' tonal quality, so that it is literally music to our ears. This is because birds –like the human voice and most musical instruments– produce few overtones. Most of the overtones produced by the equivalent of their vocal chords are filtered out in the throat and the beak.

But this is where the similarity with music ends. It is virtually impossible to translate birdsong into musical notation.

In the first place the tones, particularly those produced by songbirds, are much too high. Some birds produce sounds that are at the limit of what the human ear can hear, and sometimes even above it.

As people get older, the range of their hearing diminishes. This means that some older people can no longer hear the 'fishing reel' song of the grasshopper warbler. Musical notation also falls down when it comes to reproducing intervals,

You are more likely to hear a male oriole than to see one because it almost always sits high in the treetops to make its characteristic call.
Its name is onomatopoeic in every language: 'oriole' in English, 'wielewaal' in Dutch, 'pirol' in German and 'loriot' in French

When the sedge warbler sings it weaves different refrains together in ever-changing combinations -scratchy sounds, ticks, trills and high notes- creating lengthy songs that are different every time. A sedge warbler probably never sings the same song twice

which are much, much smaller in birdsong than they are in music made by man. And the rhythm –or its apparent absence to our ears– cannot be written down on musical staves.

Representing the sounds birds make in terms of letters and words is not very successful either, although the authors of bird guides do their best. The song of the chaffinch, for instance, by no means the most complex song, is rendered in one guide as 'chwink-chwink' and described as 'a cheery, short, vigorous succession of rather unmusical notes', while another says it is 'tsip-tsip, a delicate song ending in a flourishing pink-pink'. Anyone who is familiar with the chaffinch's song will be able to recognize something of the original in both descriptions, but whether either of them would be of any help in learning to identify the species from its song is extremely doubtful. The problem lies primarily in the consonants. We say that the cuckoo calls 'cuckoo', but the longer you listen to a cuckoo, the less you can pick out anything that sounds like a hard 'c'. It could just as easily be 'hoopoe'! The author of one field guide says that the call of the godwit is 'weeta-weeta', another describes it as 'reeka-reeka'. Many writers resort to comparisons. This produces teaspoons in glasses, objects tapping on metal

and stones sliding over ice. Well-known and very apt comparisons include the song of the European serin with stirring a bowl of broken pottery and that of the corn bunting with the jingling of a bunch of keys.

But descriptions like these are also of very limited value in learning to recognize birdsong. There is only one way to do it, and that is to get out into the field and to use your ears and eyes. Try to track down the singing bird to see which bird, what appearance belongs with the sound. When you go out on a field trip like this, it is very helpful to go with an experienced birder, who can tell you which bird is singing, even though you cannot see it. Cassettes and CDs of bird calls are also useful aids in learning to recognize the songs of different birds.

In addition to the timbre and the occurrence of certain characteristic sounds, it is the structure of the song that provides the most help in learning to distinguish and remember the different songs. If you concentrate on this aspect, you will soon discover some order in the seeming hotchpotch of sounds.

Many birds have a single, definite song, a single melody with a fixed pattern and a fixed length. The chaffinch is a good example of this. This bird sings a relatively short song, starting with a few powerful introductory notes, followed by a rattle as the central section and ending with a characteristic final flourish. If you listen carefully, you will hear that the song does not always sound exactly the same, the chaffinch makes minor variations every now and again. Most chaffinches have between three and six different versions, which vary in their details, and which they sing at random.

The song of the treecreeper, which consists of no more than a few high-pitched tones, is very simple. The 'silver laugh' of the blue tit is likewise not particularly difficult: two separate notes to start, followed by a clear trill. Other species that have a set song with a clear beginning and end include the willow warbler,

Left: The grasshopper warbler's 'fishing reel' whirring is too high-pitched for some people, particularly older people, to hear

The 'song' of the spotted flycatcher cannot really be dignified with the name. It is a relatively inconspicuous high 'see' that differs very little from its call

The dunnock's song consists of a single phrase with a fixed pattern

The song of the lesser whitethroat begins with a quiet warbling and ends with a rapid rattle on one note

The cry of the curlew is one of the most common imitations in a starling's repertoire

the redstart, the wren, the dunnock and the pied flycatcher.

In a number of species the song consists of two clearly different parts – a good aid to recognition. The blackcap, for example, starts with a warble and ends with clear, bell-like notes. The lesser whitethroat begins with a harsh, scratchy section, followed by a rapid rattle on one note. In the wood warbler, the two elements are so different that they can actually be described as two songs: a high trill beginning slowly and accelerating to a long drawn-out final note, and a melancholy piping series of 'peeoo' notes.

Then there are species which also have clearly defined songs with a beginning and an end, but longer and with more variations. The best example close to home is the blackbird. This

The characteristic call of the green sandpiper ('weet, tluitt, weet-weet') is often mimicked by starlings. It's almost impossible to tell it from the real thing!

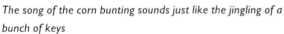
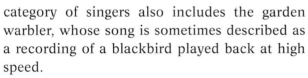

The song of the corn bunting sounds just like the jingling of a bunch of keys

The blue tit's song is a simple little trill, which has been described by poets as a 'silver laugh'

category of singers also includes the garden warbler, whose song is sometimes described as a recording of a blackbird played back at high speed.

Birds that have a repertoire of separate refrains which they can combine to their heart's content sound very different indeed. The number of refrains ranges from a few to several hundred. The most famous example of a bird with numerous notes in its song is the nightingale, to many people the 'king of the songsters'. Its song appears endlessly varied. In reality a nightingale only knows around two hundred different refrains. But because it always sings them in a different order, it succeeds in creating the impression that it never repeats itself. It does justice to all the individual elements because it never weaves them together, but always leaves brief pauses between them.

The song thrush, who does not enjoy the same fame but whose repertoire is at least as large as the nightingale's, does exactly the same thing. The difference between the song thrush and the nightingale is that the song thrush seems to enjoy the beautiful melody it has discovered so much that it likes to repeat it several times in a row, while the nightingale creates the impression of greater variety by never repeating something immediately. Other singers, like the reed warblers and the sedge warblers, use their arsenal of refrains to produce a prolonged stream of sound, in which all the elements are strung together in constantly changing combinations. The sedge warbler links scratchy sounds, clicks, trills and high chirrups together, creating lengthy songs that are different every time. A sedge warbler probably never sings the same song twice in the whole of its life.

The blue rock thrush nests on sunny cliff faces and ravines all
over Southern Europe

Immature blue rock thrush

The marsh warbler's song is likewise constantly varied, but this bird is also a master of mimicry. On average, a one-year-old male marsh warbler can imitate 77 different sounds made by other species of birds. These include African species he has heard in the winter. It is even possible that a marsh warbler's song consists entirely of imitations, but most of them escape us because we are not familiar with the 'originals'.

The marsh warbler is not the only superb mimic. The starling is another source of amusement. It is a rather 'anarchic' singer, which seems to take delight in making funny noises. Among its rattles, whistles and clicks you can frequently discover imitations of other birds. The noises starlings make will often give you a clue as to the habitat they live in or the place they have

recently been. Some mimic a lot of water birds, others imitate meadow birds. They very often do imitations of waders, like the curlew and the sandpiper – relatively simple sounds. The starling version is sometimes indistinguishable from the real thing. It is even good enough to fool members of the species being mimicked

The sweet, descending trill of the willow warbler can be heard all
day long until well into the summer

Left: Marmora's warbler sings the highest song from the top of
a bush. Marmora's warbler has a very unusual range in Europe.
It occurs almost exclusively on the islands of the western
Mediterranean: Mallorca, Corsica, Sardinia and Sicily

An olive-tree warbler in the shade of a holm oak

The lesser grey shrike occurs mainly in Southeastern Europe. Its bubbling song is very varied and includes imitations of other birds

To many people, the nightingale is the king of the songsters. Its song appears to be endlessly varied. In fact, a nightingale 'only' knows about two hundred different melodies. Because it always sings them in a different order, it creates the impression that it never repeats itself

into reacting! The biological function of this sort of mimicry has not yet been explained.

Compared with these singing superstars, the chiffchaff is no more than a pathetic simpleton. It only knows one tune, and it repeats it endlessly. The only variation is that it sometimes calls 'chiff' or 'chaff' twice in succession.

Great tits also sing simple themes of three or four notes, repeated to the point of tedium. But take care: if you listen to several great tits at the same time, you will find that they all sing differently, albeit equally simply. And if you follow an individual great tit for a while, you will realize that it too is thinking up new variations all the time. The amount of variation great tits are able to get into such a limited musical framework is nothing short of astonishing.

There are various forms of song that cannot be classified in any of these categories, like the rattles of Savi's warbler and the grasshopper warbler, the cheeping of sparrows or the cawing of crows.

Some members of the crow family can actually sing very well; it's just that they don't do it very often and the song is usually very soft. The jay is a very considerable singer, and even has quite accurate imitations in its repertoire.

The common rosefinch sings a very simple song of clear, whistling notes which, like the song of the oriole, can be recognized among thousands of others

The marsh warbler is a master mimic. On average it can imitate around eighty other species of birds, including species it has heard in its winter quarters in southern Africa

The song of the song thrush is as least as varied as the nightingale's

Previous pages: Starlings seem to enjoy making strange noises: all sorts of rattles, whistles and clicks that make their song rather anarchic. They can mimic other birds with great accuracy

The black bib is characteristic of the male Spanish sparrow. Despite its name, this species is almost entirely absent from Spain now; in Greece, on the other hand, it occurs in large numbers

Individual and geographic variation

No two birds of the same species sing exactly the same.

In most cases we would find it extremely difficult, if not impossible, to recognize these differences. But it is more than likely that the birds can hear the difference, because a female can distinguish the sound of her own mate from that of other males, young can recognize their parents by sound, and it is useful for males to be able to distinguish their neighbour's song from that of a strange intruder.

In some –although by no means all– species, geographic patterns can be detected in song variation. And in species with simple songs, we can often hear this. The song of a chaffinch in southern Europe is clearly different from that of a chaffinch in Scandinavia, which is noticeably different again from an English chaffinch.

This is not to say that there are birdsong dialects. A dialect presupposes more or less sharply-defined borders: all the birds in a particular area sing the same way, and on the other side of the border all the birds produce a different variant.

Situations like this occur very rarely in the bird world –the corn bunting is one example– and there is usually a gradual transition.

Let's take as an example a species with a repertoire of ten different songs (ten variations) and look at an individual male. The male a kilometre away probably has nine of the ten variations in common with him, a male three kilometres further away has eight, one that lives ten kilometres away will sing seven identical refrains etc.

An immature rustic bunting in its first winter - lost in Holland. Rustic buntings breed in the pine forests of Scandinavia and Siberia, and normally migrate to the southeast

The chiffchaff is quite content with the endless repetition of its own name. It occasionally relieves the monotony by calling 'chiff' or 'chaff' twice in succession

The jay's harsh screech is not its only means of expression; jays can also sing well. They sing softly, almost as though they are ashamed of it. They are also clever mimics

Juvenile male chaffinches have to learn their song. They do it in the first months of life by listening carefully to adults and learning the songs by heart. They remember them right through the winter and in the spring, after a week or two's practice, they are ready to sing with the rest

You sing to be noticed. This is why even the wren, which usually stays close to the ground in dense vegetation, sits at the top of a bush to announce its presence

How do birds learn to sing?

Young chaffinches which are reared in captivity and never hear an adult chaffinch sing produce songs that bear only a vague resemblance to a proper chaffinch's song. The songs are about the right length and cover roughly the same range of notes, but they are very simple and they lack all sorts of typical chaffinch elements. In other words, chaffinches have to learn to sing; the characteristics of the song are not innate. If the young chaffinches are played tape recordings of chaffinch song, they pick up the songs from the recordings. This means they learn from what they hear. If they grow up with another species of bird, they will adopt the song

Right: A reed bunting sings from the top of a reed

This yellowhammer has found a post so that his song will carry even further

The wheatear often looks for prominent features in the landscape

Above right: The whinchat likes open countryside, but does need a high point to sing from. This is why it can often be found in areas dotted with scrub

Right: A little bit of height is often enough. This yellow wagtail is singing from the top of a marsh marigold

of that species. Juvenile songbirds start to sing in their first spring; in the case of chaffinches this will be in February or March. First they need to practise: they sing softly, rather hesitantly. After a week or two the rehearsal phase is over and they have found the right tone. Chaffinches do not sing between August and February. This means that the young males have not been able to listen or practise for six whole months. Evidently they learn the songs they hear soon after they hatch and remember them until it is time for them to start singing themselves, months later. Two weeks are enough to practise and perfect what they have learned.

Experiments have shown that birds are most receptive to learning song in the first month after they leave the nest. In some species, hearing the song ten times is enough for them to know it, other species have to hear it several hundred times first. This is not really all that many: an adult songbird can produce that number of songs in just a few hours. In most species the young are independent of the parents within a week or two of leaving the nest. This means that they probably do not learn song from their father, although this would seem to be the most obvious thing to do. Despite a great number of experiments, virtually no evidence has been found to suggest that song is learned from the parents.

Where do birds sing?

A singing bird wants to let its presence be known and announce its location, preferably over a fairly great distance. This is why most birds choose a high, conspicuous place from which to sing. Even birds that usually hide away in dense bushes, like the wren, robin and

Above left: This skylark is sitting on a post to sing, but skylarks usually sing on the wing, remaining in the air for minutes at a time

Left and above: At the end of its song-flight the meadow pipit descends like a parachutist and lands on a post, where it sometimes carries on singing

dunnock, or generally skulk on the ground, like the yellowhammer, are now out in the open at the top of a tree or bush. Blackbirds and redstarts in towns call out from the rooftops. Songbirds of the open fields, such as the wheatear, the stonechat and the whinchat, choose a prominent feature of the landscape: a rock, a bush, the top of a sturdy thistle, a fence or a post. From an elevated, open position like this, you not only put your own message across more effectively, it is also easier to hear other birds' messages.

By doing this, birds do of course make themselves vulnerable. It makes them very easy for birds of prey to locate. Whereas they spend the rest of their lives doing their utmost to minimize the risk of being caught, the importance of successful reproduction –because that's what

this is all about– evidently outweighs the danger. The high perch also makes it easier for the birds to see trouble coming.

For some birds, even a treetop is not high enough, and they sing in flight. The skylark hangs in the air singing for minutes at a time. The woodlark also sings for long periods in flight. Each time it sings one of its characteristic melancholy, descending melodies, the bird itself also descends. This coincidence of flight and song is also found among the pipits, like the meadow pipit and the tree pipit.

As the bird climbs, it produces an accelerating, rising note. Then it descends, with a descending and decelerating song, floating like a hang-glider with outstretched wings. The sedge warbler and the whitethroat have a habit of suddenly ascending from a reedbed or bush halfway through their song and singing a phrase or two -lasting no more than a few seconds- in the air, before dropping back into cover again.

Birdsong all year round

In the spring, the birds' chorus swells to full strength. Of course this is related to the functions of birdsong I discussed in chapter 1: establishing territories and mating. As the spring progresses, the ranks of the avian choir are reinforced as all the migrants that have overwintered elsewhere start to trickle back again. Most birds become less vocal as soon as they have started breeding, so song activity starts to tail off towards the end of June. After a quiet period in the hottest summer months, it picks up again slightly in the late summer. But it is never completely silent, even in the winter. Birds can be heard singing in every month of the year.

The early morning is by far the best time for birdsong

Winter

In the first couple of months of the year the permanent residents and the birds who have returned to the breeding sites early (because they did not migrate very far) have things all to themselves. On bright, sunny mornings in January, the great tit and the blue tit are already in full song. Here and there a group of starlings can be heard chattering at the top of a tree and a chorus of sparrows sits chirping in a gutter. The treecreeper and the goldcrest are also vocal in the depths of winter. The first blackbirds start singing – rather softly and hesitantly. These are probably the previous year's juveniles that still have to practise. This whispering song of young birds is called 'subsong'. The song thrush and mistle thrush –migrants who do not go very far– also start to sing early, in January or February. At the end of February, the chaffinch joins the company. In the following weeks, we experience the peak in the song activity of the dunnock and the marsh tit.

Spring

During March, the chiffchaff is the first of the summer visitors among the songbirds to return, soon followed by the willow warbler. Then all the summer birds start to come back from Southern Europe and Africa: the blackcap, lesser whitethroat, redstart, pied flycatcher, wood warbler, sedge warbler, reed warbler, garden warbler and marsh warbler. They start to sing at full power almost immediately they arrive at their breeding sites, so in April there are new sounds to hear practically every day. This continues until well into May. The spotted flycatcher and, in the easternmost part of the country, the golden oriole are the last to join the songbirds' chorus. Meanwhile, some of the

Left: The blue tit's trill can be heard in January

Starlings will start singing on fine, sunny days in winter

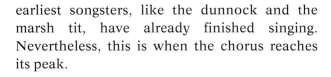

Goldcrests sing very early in the year

Mistle thrushes do not migrate very far and are back at their nest sites very early in the year. They soon start to sing, well before most of the other songbirds

earliest songsters, like the dunnock and the marsh tit, have already finished singing. Nevertheless, this is when the chorus reaches its peak.

Summer

As we get into June, the song tails off rapidly, although the willow warbler, yellowhammer and whitethroat will carry on for some considerable time yet. Most birds sing busily during the period from their arrival at the breeding site until the moment the eggs are laid. After this they sing less frequently, with brief revivals at dawn and occasionally at dusk. Male sedge warblers actually stop singing altogether as soon as they have formed an established pair with a female.

July and August are the quietest months. Most

songbirds have finished breeding and started the moult. During this period you could be forgiven for thinking that they have vanished off the face of the earth. Most of the summer visitors head off silently to their winter quarters; the odd one may let fly with a snatch of song on the way. At the end of August, for example, you can sometimes hear the rattle of the lesser whitethroat.

Autumn

The willow warbler, chiffchaff and black redstart suddenly burst into song again in September and October. The reasons for this autumn song are not entirely clear. Some people say that it is the young birds singing at this time, but this is at most only partly true. It is primarily the adults of these species that sing.

It is possible that they are defending feeding territories during this period. This is certainly the motive behind the robins' singing, which can be heard in full flood in these months. In fact, like the indefatigable wrens, they never really stop singing at any time of the year.

In the short, dark days around the turn of the year and during periods of frost it can be uncannily quiet. But it takes just the slightest improvement in the weather to start the harbingers of spring –the tits, starlings and thrushes– off again.

Birdsong around the clock

In the breeding season –from April until early June– birdsong can be heard in every hour out of the twenty-four. The greatest concentration of song is the dawn chorus, which starts up half an hour before sunrise and continues for two hours afterwards. Some birds, blackbirds for example, only really do their best for a quarter of an hour or so, whereas others sing on tirelessly.

There is a shorter performance, involving fewer performers, in the evening. All sorts of explanations have been put forward for why birds

The reed warbler is one of the many summer visitors that are not heard until the end of April, when they return from Africa

The song of the whinchat is heard mainly in May and June. It is a real summer visitor, spending its winters in the heart of Africa

sing mainly in the morning. Sound carries further in the morning; it is the least suitable time to look for food; the females arrive at the breeding sites at night; the females are at their most fertile in the morning. In other words there are several possible reasons, but no single satisfactory explanation.

Dawn

If you want to enjoy birdsong at its most impressive, you will have to get up early. Pick a fine morning in May, when the weather is dry and not too cold, and there is not a lot of wind. Choose an area where there are lots of birds, for instance a mixed wood with open spaces. You

will undoubtedly have an unforgettable experience. If you don't want to miss the beginning of
the concert, you will have to be out at least an
hour before dawn. It will still be completely
dark. Ahead of all the other birds, the first redstart breaks the silence with its short, characteristic refrain. The plaintive notes of the first
robin soon follow. As the darkness starts to
waver and dissolve, about three-quarters of an
hour before the sun rises, the blackbird and
song thrush join in. For a little while, less than
half an hour, all the blackbirds sing together.

Wrens sing all year round

*The black redstart (the bird in the picture is a female) suddenly
starts singing again in September and October*

*The song of the redstart often rings out in the early morning,
when it is still dark and all the other birds are silent*

*Following pages: The yellowhammer is tireless. It carries on
singing until late in the summer*

The first robin starts singing an hour before sunrise

In the last half hour before dawn, as one blackbird after another falls silent, almost all the other species come in: wrens, great tits and blue tits, chiffchaffs, blackcaps and garden warblers. Just as the sun rises, the chaffinch and the wood warbler join the chorus, which is now at greatest strength. Even later, when the earliest songsters are calling it a day, the pied flycatcher at last strikes up.

Late morning and afternoon

In the course of the morning, the chorus diminishes. By the afternoon it seems as though all the birds have disappeared from the woods apart from a few chaffinches stubbornly singing away. There is more going on in open spaces. Even in the heat of the midday sun, the skylark and woodlark continue to sing, as do the tree pipit, yellowhammer, linnet and whitethroat.

Below: the blackcap is one of the many songbirds that start to sing in the last half-hour before dawn and carry on in full flood for the next two or three hours

The great blackbird chorus rings out in the first light of dawn. Just briefly, all the blackbirds sing together

Right: Linnets sing at all hours of the day

A skylark can even be heard singing on hot summer afternoons

Left: Female pied flycatcher. Polygamy, in other words a male (below) with a number of females (usually two) is quite common among pied flycatchers

Following pages: After a peak in the morning, the song thrush bursts into full song again around sunset. Its song rings through the woods on mild, windless evenings

Evening and night

The chorus picks up again in the evening as most species make themselves heard again. At this time of the day, fewer birds take part than in the early morning, and the chorus does not last anything like as long.

As dusk falls, the principal singers are the song thrush, the blackbird and the robin. It is never totally silent. At night, an individual nightingale will do justice to his name, and you will occa-sionally hear the marsh warbler, grasshopper warbler and woodlark.

The song is affected by the weather conditions. On cold, windy or rainy mornings, few birds feel like singing. If the sun breaks through later, a lot of birds will start singing in the middle of the day.

Thrushes and robins like to sing in mild, wind-less, damp weather, even in a drizzle, particu-larly in the evening.

Why do birds sing so early?

All sorts of answers have been suggested to the question as to why birds sing mainly in the early morning. It could be a sort of morning roll-call, with all the territory holders announcing that they are still there. It is thought that most bird deaths happen at night, so that the morning would be the best time for males who are still

looking for a territory to move into a site that has become vacant. The morning might also be the best time to find a female. Many songbirds migrate at night, which means that the females arrive at the breeding site during the night. This explanation is not really satisfactory, since species which migrate during the day, like the finches, also sing primarily in the morning, and the song continues to be concentrated in the morning even after the females have arrived. The females may very well be an important

The tree pipit sings doggedly on throughout the day

The woodlark sings its clear melodious song day and night

A female redstart: Some people suggest that birds tend to sing in the mornings because the females arrive at the nesting sites during the night. Another explanation is that the females are at their most fertile in the morning, so this is when it makes sense for males to do their best

The whirring sound of the grasshopper warbler can sometimes also be heard at night

factor, but in a very different way. They generally lay eggs early in the morning, and immediately afterwards they are at their most fertile. It is possible that the males sing at precisely this time in order to 'reserve' their mates for themselves. One significant advantage of the early morning could be that sound carries better then. What's more, there are few other sounds at that time of the day. This benefit would appear to be cancelled out because all the birds sing at once. But it seems that birds avoid competing with one another. Species that sing in the same frequency range make sure that they do not sing at the same time. They listen to one another, and use one another's pauses.

And lastly, the morning is not such a good time to look for food. This would apply particularly to the insect-eaters; their prey is less active in the early morning than it is later in the day and it is harder to find in the half-light. It is therefore most efficient to spend the morning singing and the rest of the day looking for food.

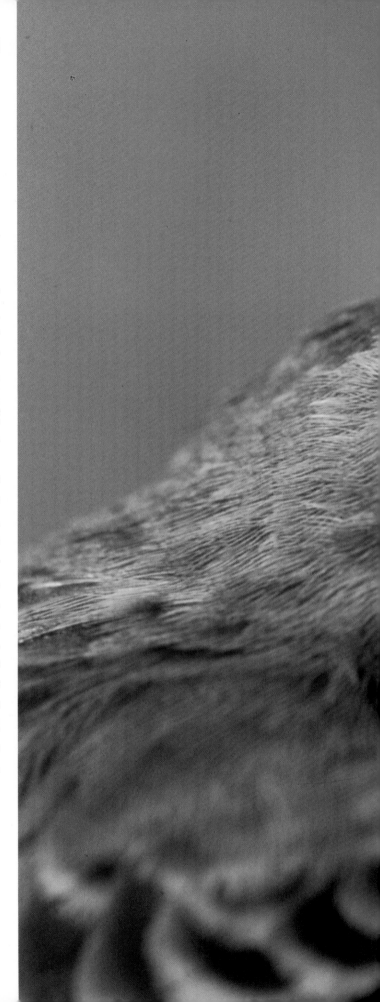

CHAPTER 4

Songbirds in their habitat

Songbirds seem to have been made for a life among trees and bushes. And, indeed, most species of songbirds do live in wooded areas, where few other groups of species can follow them. But we find songbirds in almost every conceivable environment. No other group of birds is so widespread over so many sorts of terrain. In this chapter I shall look at the principal types of landscape in Europe and the songbirds that live there.

The survey starts close to home. Some species, like the house sparrow, have adapted to man and are now only found in the vicinity of people. But songbirds can also be found in the most inhospitable polar regions and in the perpetual snows of the high mountains. The hot, dry steppes of Southern and Eastern Europe, with their sparse vegetation, shrivelled to nothing in the summer, are home to a surprising number of species of songbirds. Woodlands have more songbirds, but the greatest numbers and the greatest variety of species are found in varied landscapes where woodland, scrub and open areas are interspersed.

The rock pipit is one of the very few songbirds to nest mainly on rocky shorelines

Followers of civilization

The closest songbirds to us are our 'tenants' – birds that use buildings as their nest sites. House sparrows and starlings nest under roof tiles and in all sorts of nooks and crannies. They have thrown in their lot with man; these birds do not live in places where there are no people, but wherever there are people, there they are too.

The pied wagtail and swallow are real followers of civilization who use structures created by man for their nests.

Less striking and less familiar, but equally typ-ical, is the black redstart. Originally a mountain-dweller, in the south of Europe it is still found mainly in the mountains.

In Western and Central Europe it lives in cities and towns, where it has discovered an excellent substitute for real rocks in houses, factories and other buildings.

The house martin has made a similar exchange of real for surrogate. Originally it built its mud nest under an overhanging ledge of rock, but nowadays house martins nest mainly under the eaves and gutters of buildings, in colonies ranging in size from a few nests to many hundreds.

A built-up area with vegetation makes an attractive nest site for many songbirds

The black redstart was originally a mountain bird, but it is now found mainly in towns and cities. It has discovered that buildings make an excellent substitute for rock faces when it comes to building a nest

A pair of house martins gathers mud for their nest, which the birds are attaching to a wall under the eaves of the roof

Birds of the tundra and mountains

There is one songbird that lives far from the inhabited world, in some of the most inhospitable spots you could imagine. This is the snow bunting. It nests in the extreme north of Europe, on rocky coasts, on mountain tops and in the stony tundra. In its and white summer plumage it blends in perfectly in this world of snow, ice and bare rock. In areas where the tundra is not quite as harsh, we find the Lapland bunting. Both the snow bunting and the Lapland bunting take advantage of the abundance of insects in the brief polar summer and live on seeds for the rest of the year. Both species are to be found on the coasts of Britain and Western Europe in the winter, like a third resident of the tundra and fells, the shore lark. With the shore lark we move to that other bleak, inhospitable world of rock and snow, the high mountains. In the Balkans and in Turkey this is the habitat where we encounter the shore

A snow bunting in the tundra in summer. Despite the flourishing monkshood the surroundings look quite comfortable, but snow buntings can and do live in the most inhospitable spots

lark again. High in the Alps, above 2000 metres, we find a sort of double of the snow bunting: the snow finch. They are not actually related, but are remarkably alike in appearance, voice and behaviour.

Other species of songbirds live above the tree line in the Alps and the mountain ranges of Southern Europe, among them the alpine accentor, water pipit and wallcreeper. The crow family is also represented, mainly by the alpine chough, which is only ever found in the high mountains. Alpine choughs are real aerial acrobats, who use the eddying air currents around mountain peaks and rock faces for their formation stunt flying. At the same time they make noises reminiscent of a pinball machine. The yellow beak and red legs complete the clown-like effect.

Left: A snow bunting in its winter plumage on the coast of Western Europe

The Lapland bunting is another typical bird of the tundra. It nests in less hostile areas, with more vegetation, than the snow bunting

The shore lark is found on the tundra of Scandinavia and in the high mountains of the Balkans and Turkey. Like the snow buntings, the tundra birds overwinter along the coast of Western Europe

The related chough, with red legs and a red beak, takes over from the alpine chough on the rocky shorelines of the west coasts of Britain and Ireland.
The only small songbird in these areas is the rock pipit.

Water-dwellers

There is one true water bird among the European songbirds – the dipper. It can dive, swim and walk under water along the river bed to catch insects. It is a typical inhabitant of the fast-flowing water of streams and small rivers,

Many mountaineers are familiar with the snow finch. It is an extremely tame little bird, which is totally unafraid of people and will allow you to approach very close

The alpine accentor nests high in the Alps and the mountains of Southern Europe

The water pipit breeds high in the mountains and spends the winter in the lowlands. This individual is in its winter plumage

preferably with stones and rocks. It builds its nest in a rock crevice at the water's edge. The grey wagtail nests in the same surroundings, but does not venture into the water. Instead it picks up insects from the surface of the water or catches them along the banks.

Reedbed and marsh birds

Songbirds are much more numerous and varied in the reedbeds around lakes and reservoirs.

The bearded tit can be found there all year round, feeding on insects in the summer and seeds in the winter.

The reed bunting is a permanent resident of reedy banks and marshes. In the summer it has the company of reed warblers and sedge warblers who have spent the winter in tropical Africa. The great reed warbler and the reed warbler build beautiful cup-shaped, suspended

Following pages: The high mountains far above the tree line are the domain of the snow finch

The alpine chough is the aerial acrobat of the mountains. Flocks of alpine choughs use the thermals around the tops of mountains and cliffs to perform their stunt flying. At the same time they make noises like a pinball machine. The yellow beak and red legs complete the clown-like image

Fast-running water: the habitat of the dipper

*Left: The dipper is the only true water bird among the songbirds.
It can dive, swim and walk along the stream bed under the water*

*Right: The grey wagtail occupies the same habitat as the dipper:
fast-flowing rivers and mountain streams. It finds its food
between the stones at the water's edge*

nests, which they attach to a couple of reed
stems.
The sedge warbler and Savi's warbler nest on or
close to the ground.

Meadow birds

The open fields are the domain of the skylark,
meadow pipit and yellow wagtail. They are
found in grassland –natural or man-made–
heaths and moors, and arable land. They build
their nests on the ground, well hidden among
the tussocks of grass. The wheatear often nests

A marshland habitat: the Oostvaarders lakes in Holland

Below: Bearded tits are very much birds of the reedbeds. The male is on the left and the female on the right

under the ground in rabbit holes, but will also use holes and cracks between rocks and similar sites.

There are even more species of songbirds in the dry plains of Southern and Eastern Europe, thanks mainly to the abundant food supplies in these apparently barren areas. They support a great many annual plants which produce a great deal of seed, and they are also home to huge numbers of the larger insects such as beetles, grasshoppers and crickets.

The lark family is particularly well represented in the songbird population here. The crested lark occurs in the greatest numbers and the calandra lark is the largest. Then there are the short-toed lark, the lesser short-toed lark and in Spain, the heartland for plains birds, we also find the Thekla lark and Dupont's lark.

Where the open plain is dotted here and there with bushes, we can look out for whinchats and stonechats. They nest on the ground, but often sit at the top of a bush or other prominent feature to sing. Scattered trees in a dry, bare landscape often attract woodlarks.

Birds of scrub and hedgerows

From the regions with scattered trees we move to the areas of denser trees and bushes where

Several of the larks breed in the fields and plains of Southern Europe. The crested lark is the most common

The meadow pipit has a decided preference for open country-side. Any sort of grassland, including farmland, will do

The wheatear lives in open, grassy habitats and nests in rock crevices and rabbit holes

This photograph shows just how long the grey wagtail's tail actually is

A great reed warbler near the nest

The great reed warbler's nest is a perfect bowl, attached to a couple of sturdy reeds

The calandra lark is the largest species of lark in the arid grasslands and farmland of the south and east of Europe. The greatest numbers are to be found in Spain and Russia

the songbirds have a virtual monopoly –at least in the bird world– and where they are the most notable inhabitants.

Many songbirds prefer places with plenty of bushes, but few if any high trees.

If possible they avoid open areas, but they do not like woodland either. We find them in the scrub on the sunny fringes of woods, in the bushes and young trees in clearings or in fens and marshes with dense growths of willow and birch. This is where the nightingale, the blue-throat, the marsh warbler, the grasshopper warbler, the whitethroat, the willow warbler, the red-backed shrike and the linnet are at home.

For some of these birds the hedgerows and thickets that surround the fields in some parts of Europe are a good alternative. The yellow-hammer is in its element here, too.

There are many scrubland birds to be found among the hills and slopes of the countries around the Mediterranean, with their vegeta-

The bluethroat likes scrub with open areas and no high trees

The black-eared wheatear is one of the most common species found in the maquis and garigue around the Mediterranean. This is a male

Spain is principal habitat of the short-toed lark, which likes bone-dry ground with sparse vegetation

tion of maquis and garigue. The low dense scrub with numerous thorn bushes is paradise for the black-eared wheatear, Dartford warbler, subalpine warbler, Sardinian warbler, Orphean warbler, woodchat shrike and cirl bunting. The small-scale agriculture here, which creates a mosaic of little fields, orchards and copses, provides an attractive habitat for many songbird species.

Woodland birds

And lastly we arrive in the woods, where the greatest variety of songbirds is to be found – always provided, that is, that the wood meets all the criteria. What these are becomes clear when we look at the places in the wood in which we find songbirds.

By no means all songbirds are to be found among the leaves of trees and bushes. Several species, including the chiffchaff and wood warbler, build carefully concealed nests on the woodland floor. Others, like the dunnock, blackcap and garden warbler, nest close to the ground in a dense bush. The chaffinch nests in the fork of a branch and the goldcrest suspends

The subalpine warbler is numerous in maquis in the countries around the Mediterranean. It likes to hide in dense, prickly bushes

Below: The willow tit nests in natural holes, often close to the ground, for example in rotten tree stumps

You can see the woodchat shrike in maquis and semi-open countryside in the south of Europe

The cirl bunting likes dry, sunny maquis slopes around the Mediterranean. Its monotonous rattle and the chirping of crickets are inextricably linked with hot summer days when the air shimmers

its nest under the foliage of an evergreen. And then there are the many songbirds that nest in holes. Some of them, such as the nuthatch, prefer to nest in hollow trees, while others, including the spotted flycatcher and the coal tit, usually nest lower down, for instance in a rotten tree trunk.

Each species also has its own area in which to hunt for food. The robin, blackbird and song thrush forage on the ground. Tits and tree-creepers find insects and spiders in cracks and crevices in branches and twigs. The blackcap and the garden warbler hunt for insects and small invertebrates on the surface of leaves. And flycatchers catch insects in the air.

Most species need a combination of different places. The chiffchaff nests on the ground, but finds its food among the leaves of trees and bushes. The song thrush nests in a bush, but forages on the ground. The redstart nests in hollow trees, but often hunts for food on the woodland floor. The robin usually nests and forages on or close to the ground, but, like most birds, looks for a vantage point high in a bush or tree in order to sing.

This means that a wood with lots of birds is a varied wood. A wood is often described as having three vertical layers: the tree canopy, the undergrowth and the ground cover. All three layers must be well developed in order to house a varied songbird population. The more variation, the more birds: variation in tall and low trees and variation in open and dense spots. There also has to be dead wood around for the hole-nesters.

The ancient woodland that covered huge areas of Europe in the distant past met all these criteria. Storms, floods and insect depredation created clearings where the sunlight could penetrate to the forest floor again and where young trees and bushes seized their opportunity. Dead wood remained where it fell and in turn attracted new life. This natural woodland has now all but completely disappeared. Its place has been taken by planted forests, most of which are managed for timber production.

A great spotted woodpecker near its nest hole. The holes made by woodpeckers are reused by other hole-nesters like the nuthatch

The nuthatch is a hole-nester found mainly in old woodland. It does not make a hole for itself; instead it uses a natural hole or an old woodpecker's nest. It makes the entrance smaller by plastering it up with mud, to keep larger species from annexing the hole

These woods and forests have less to offer songbirds. Most of them are fairly uniform, divided into blocks of trees of a single species and the same age, planted in neat rows.

A large proportion of the forests that have been planted are coniferous, even in areas where conifers are not indigenous. Conifers are easy to grow, even in poor soil. A coniferous forest supports relatively few birds. It is dense and dark, so very little grows on the forest floor. On the other hand, some songbirds, including the coal tit, the crested tit, the goldcrest, the siskin and the crossbill, are specifically tied to conifers. These birds have been able to extend their range significantly thanks to the spread of coniferous woods and forests.

The loss of natural biotope is offset to some extent by an expansion of substitute habitats in the shape of parks and gardens. Many originally woodland birds are now common there. The blackbird, song thrush, robin, wren, dunnock, chiffchaff, blackcap, garden warbler, spotted flycatcher and pied flycatcher, great tit, blue tit, long-tailed tit and chaffinch are all woodland and forest birds that have adapted. Some

The coal tit is one of the species at home in a pinewood

Right: The range of different planting makes parks an attractive alternative to woods for many songbirds

species are actually more numerous in these man-made surroundings than they are in the woods. This is not really surprising. Most species need variety, and the vegetation in man's environment provides much more than a dull managed forest. Nevertheless, the woods are the first choice for species when it really comes down to it.

It has been established, for instance, that the great tit and the blue tit, which would appear at first glance to be real garden birds, successfully rear more young in the woods than they do in gardens. If the wren population has been hard hit during a severe winter, they will have disappeared from gardens, but they will still be in the woods. 'City blackbirds' on the other hand, are more successful than 'woodland blackbirds' thanks to the extra food and the kinder microclimate.

CHAPTER 5

The life of song-birds

In this chapter we look at the life of songbirds in terms of an annual cycle. The first phase in the life of birds is the breeding season, which begins with the establishment of territory and mating, and ends when the young fly the nest. Then comes the moult, migration and survival through the winter.

These phases, like many of the aspects we shall be dealing with in the various stages, are not specific to songbirds, but apply to the life of birds in general. As far as reproduction is concerned, songbirds have several other things in common in addition to the role of song we discussed in previous chapters. They all take great care in building their nests; they all have the ability to build complex nests; they are able to produce a great many offspring every year, among other things by rearing several broods; and all young songbirds are hatched out in the nest and have to grow up in the nest.

There are all sorts of exceptions to this general pattern among the songbirds. But in the scope of this book, we only have space to mention a few of them.

Baby house sparrows beg their father for food. After they have flown, the juveniles are still looked after by the parents for another two or three weeks

A song thrush's nest

A long-tailed tit with food for its brood. You can get an awful lot of insects in one beak

Previous pages: Sand martins dig nest holes in vertical walls of sand or loam, for example river banks and sandpits. Behind the opening there is a tunnel 50 to 100 cm long with a nest chamber at the end. When the young are twelve days old they come to the opening to be fed. Sand martins nest in colonies which can sometimes contain hundreds of pairs

tunnel anything from half a metre to a metre long with a nest compartment at the end. When the young are twelve days old, they make their own way to the entrance for feeding.

The long-tailed tit and penduline tit take about three weeks to build their extremely intricate nests. The robin, which puts together an untidy structure on the ground, is finished in three or four days. The blackbird comes between these two with a construction time of ten to fourteen days. In most species, the male and female build the nest together. Once a pair of great tits or blue tits have decided on the nest box in your garden, you will see both partners flying in and out with tufts of moss, bits of straw and other material for the nest.

The swallows, too, build their nest in the shed together.

The blackbirds' nest in the hedge, in contrast, is all the work of the female, while among wrens it is the male who does the whole job.

Colony birds

The house martin and the sand martin are the most characteristic colony nesters among the European songbirds. Their colonies can number many hundreds of breeding pairs, and there is often very little distance between the nests. In fact, house martin nests are sometimes stuck

A nest containing two hungry young orioles. When the chicks hear one of the parents approaching they automatically open their beaks wide to show the brightly coloured interior. This stimulates the parents to put food in

Seed eaters like this reed bunting feed their young mainly on animal protein. It contains all the necessary nutrients and is usually in plentiful supply in the summer

The parents have a full-time job feeding their brood. The male and the female both fly back and forth constantly. This is a pair of yellowhammers: the male above and the female below

one on another. Evidently territorial behaviour is not a factor where these birds are concerned. The sparrows and some of the finches nest in colonies, but they are generally smaller and much more loose-knit. Typical of sparrows are the small colonies –sometimes of several species– under storks' nests.

The Spanish sparrow can form very large, close colonies. There are also a number of species in the crow family that nest in colonies, including the jackdaw (a hole-nester), the alpine chough and the chough (which nest in rocks). Their colonies are usually small, often just a few pairs. The rook, which often breeds in very large colonies, builds its nest at the top of high trees. Sixteen thousand nests were once counted in a rookery in Hungary! This is exceptional, however, and colonies of more than a thousand pairs usually consist of a number of separate sub-colonies or 'branches'.

Eggs

Once the nest is finished, the female can start to lay eggs. The number of eggs varies from species to species, but is usually somewhere between three and seven. A tit's nest can contain as many as twelve eggs. In the great tit and the blue tit the number is very variable; sometimes they may lay no more than five. The long-tailed tit and coal tit lay at least seven or eight eggs. Birds gear the number of eggs to their circumstances. When food is plentiful they lay more eggs than they do when food is scarce.

The female lays an egg every day. She does not start to incubate the eggs until the brood is complete. This ensures that all the eggs hatch at roughly the same time. In many songbirds only the female sits on the eggs; in some species the male takes over from her now and then, but the female always does the lion's share.

Young

After about two weeks of incubation, the young bird hatches out of the egg. Young songbirds are born naked, blind and helpless. At first they need their parents to keep them warm. The

Right: Juvenile swallows are fed by their parents for a few weeks after they leave the nest. The parent pushes the food into the youngster's beak on the wing. The whole operation is over in an instant

A short-lived glut: a swarm of mayflies. Birds rear their young in the summer because there is a good supply of food at this time of the year

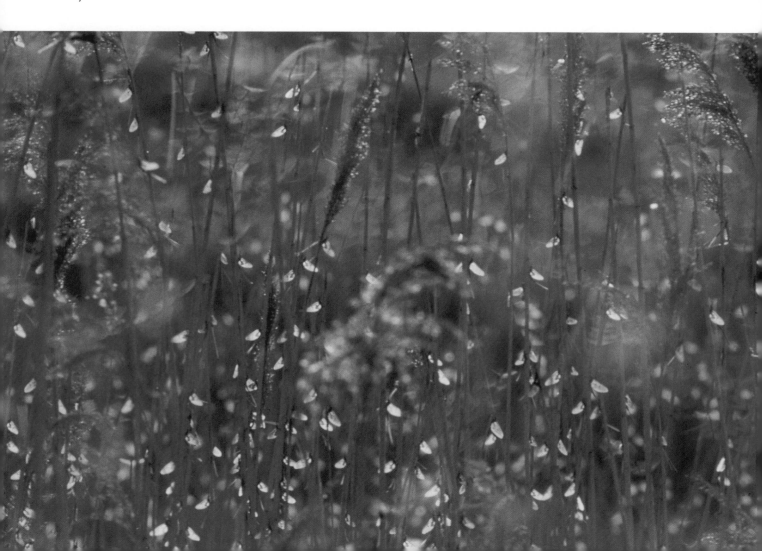

parents have a full-time job feeding the young. They fly in and out constantly, with the male doing his share. If all goes well, the young will hatch at a time when there is plenty of their special food to be had. In almost all songbirds, this food consists of insects and other invertebrates. Even birds that are otherwise confirmed seed-eaters, like the finches and the buntings, feed their young on this type of food because it contains more of the nutrients required for growth.

When one of the parents lands on the nest, the young birds automatically open their brightly coloured beaks wide and start begging for food as loudly as they can. The parent bird makes no effort to share the food out fairly, it simply shoves it into the nearest gaping beak. This means that the greediest member of the brood

An immature redstart. Never, ever pick up a 'poor abandoned' juvenile. They really are being looked after by their parents

A young rose-coloured starling grows like a weed. At the top: the bird is about five days old. Below: it is around fifteen days old

The young birds hatch at the moment when their most important source of food is abundant. For the great tit it is the caterpillar

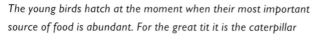

Most songbirds are not long-lived. Here a Montagu's harrier has caught a blackbird

gets most. Once it is satisfied, it stops begging and another of the young gets its share. Ultimately all the baby birds get enough, provided that there is plenty of food around. If there is not enough, only the strongest will make it. This is a hard but effective way of ensuring that the species has the best possible chance of survival.

When the parent bird leaves the nest it takes the droppings produced by the young with it, often packaged in a sort of membrane. This is a hygienic measure which helps to prevent disease in the nest and means that there are no traces of white to attract the attention of marauding predators.

Flying the nest

The juveniles leave the nest a week or two after they hatch. The strongest one may fly a couple of days earlier than the weakest brother or sister. Immature songbirds can fly right away,

without any practice. This is quite remarkable, because young birds that have been raised in a hole in a tree or a nest box have never even been able to spread their wings before! Just at first, however, they are not very good at manoeuvring and landing. Young garden birds are an easy prey for cats at this stage. Once a juvenile has landed safely on a branch near the nest, it immediately starts begging for food. The young stay with their parents for two or three weeks and are fed until they are completely independent. At that moment the family ceases to exist. The parents will no longer tolerate their young in their territory; the juveniles fly off in search of a place of their own. This is known as 'dispersion'.

The young often remain within a couple of kilometres of the place where they were hatched, but it is not that unusual for them to move a hundred kilometres or more. This is a mechanism for regulating population density,

Autumn. By the time the leaves turn, most of the migrants to Africa are already long gone. Other species that do not have so far to go start moving now

In autumn and winter great tits, which are essentially insect eaters, eat a great many seeds, such as beech nuts and peanuts

In the autumn, the blackbird supplements its diet of earthworms and insects with berries

with the older birds occupying the best sites while the young have to prove themselves elsewhere. It also means that they can discover good new areas by chance.

Several broods

One of the reasons why the parents no longer have any time for their young is that they are already breeding again themselves. Almost all songbirds that start nesting early in the season and have enough time left will produce a second brood. The blackbird and the house sparrow can actually rear as many as four broods in a single season. The only species to stop at one brood are some of the migratory birds which do not get back until late in the spring, such as the garden warbler, the icterine warbler and the reed warbler.

It is vital to rear as many young as possible. Songbirds are not long-lived – their average life expectancy is no more than a year or two. It is quite normal for ninety percent of young birds to die in their first year. Birds need a hefty 'reserve' to compensate for this staggering death rate.

It is particularly important for the permanent residents to have a long breeding season: by producing extra broods they can make up for the huge losses after a hard winter. It means that the population of a species like the wren can recover from a severe setback in just a couple of years.

The moult

Once the breeding season is over, the moult begins. The birds' plumage will have suffered during the hard work of breeding. Feathers are dead things that cannot repair themselves, so they have to be replaced. This happens at least once a year. Most songbirds change all their plumage in late summer. This is one of the few quiet moments in a bird's life. They are not called upon for any other major effort, such as breeding or migrating, and there is plenty of food around.

What's more, the new plumage is ready in time to withstand the long journey or survive the cold winter.

The moult itself is taxing enough: it takes a great deal of energy to grow new feathers. The moult is also a dangerous period, because the birds cannot fly as well and are consequently an easier prey for predators. During this period –which lasts about five weeks for most species– songbirds tend to keep their heads down; they

Bearded tits switch from insects to reed seeds in winter

stay under cover as much as possible and make very little noise.

During this period the migrants also start to eat more so as to lay down a reserve of fat for the long journey. Many of the insect eaters supplement their diet with berries at this time. Berries are plentiful now and ideal for putting on extra weight.

Migration

August marks the start of the migration. The insect eaters leave first, before the autumn really sets in, at a moment when there is still enough food. Were they to leave any later they would run the risk of not being able to find enough food on the way, during the migration. The date on which these birds leave is determined genetically and governed by hormonal changes, triggered primarily by the shortening length of the days. Species that collect insects from leaves or catch them on the wing, like the sedge warbler, whitethroat, garden warbler, willow warbler and flycatcher, set out particularly early. Most of them spend the winter in tropical Africa. They leave in a fixed order – each species at the moment when their innate migratory urge tells them to go. You will barely notice this mass movement of birds unless you specifically look out for it. Most of the birds leave at night, because they have to eat during the day. What's more, they do not form flocks; each individual leaves separately, so they are not noticeable. The swallow family (swallows, house martins and sand martins) are an exception in both respects. Weeks before they leave they start gathering together in an ever larger flock. They leave during the day, and feed on the wing as they travel.

The most important source of food for siskins in the winter: alder catkins. In this case the food is encased in ice and inaccessible. Birds have a hard time of it in conditions like these

Insect eaters like the robin are almost never seen more than singly in the winter. They have a better chance of surviving the winter if they stay on their own, because their food is widely dispersed and often difficult to find. This is why robins defend their feeding territories in the winter

In some years there are mass invasions of waxwings. They happen when a shortage of food forces the birds to move outside their normal range. They can turn up anywhere there are berries, even in city gardens. Invasions are a phenomenon of birds whose food may be plentiful one year and scarce the next

In the course of September, when most of the summer songsters have gone, the migration of the seed eaters (finches, buntings, larks and thrushes) gets under way. These birds migrate much less far, certainly no farther than the south of Europe. Their movements are much more obvious because they leave during the day in flocks.

In the autumn and winter many of the insect eaters supplement their diet with berries and seeds or switch to a completely vegetarian diet. At this time of the year thrushes eat a lot of berries, tits often eat beech nuts and the bearded tit switches to reed seeds.

Long-distance travellers

Migrating songbirds, particularly the species that fly to Africa, achieve an amazing feat. There are countless risks on the way and a great many of the birds do not survive the journey. Nevertheless the rewards make the effort worth while, otherwise birds would never embark on

it. Staying in the breeding area brings with it the very real danger of a shortage of food, particularly in severe winters. This also costs many birds their lives, particularly young and inexperienced ones. Birds weigh up the costs of going or staying. Depending on their habitat, the type of food and its availability, in one species the scales will come down on the side of going, while in others the advantages of staying will tip the balance.

In order to survive a migration of thousands, sometimes tens of thousands of kilometres, songbirds lay down reserves of fat before they leave. In the long-distance fliers these reserves are considerable, so that they can almost double their normal weight. In theory, at least, this enables birds like the whitethroat and garden warbler to fly across the Mediterranean and the Sahara without stopping!

As well as these physical reserves, birds also have an innate 'feeling' for the right direction for migration and an extraordinary ability,

The special shape of the bill, with its crossed mandibles, lets the crossbill dig the seeds out of pine cones. Unfortunately, conifers have the annoying habit of producing huge amounts of seed one year, and very little the next. This is why crossbills undertake great treks looking for areas where the food supply is good. They are true nomads with no fixed abode

which is still largely a riddle to us, to orientate and remain on course. They steer by the sun, the stars at night and the earth's magnetism. You can read more about the migration of birds in the book 'Migratory Birds in Europe', which has also been published in this series.

Overwintering

Songbirds that spend the winter here are insect eaters that find their food on the ground (robin, wren, blackbird) or dig it out from cracks and splits in branches and trunks (tits, treecreeper, nuthatch), species that live on seeds and berries in the winter (redwing, fieldfare, great tit, blue tit, chaffinch, brambling, siskin) and omnivores (carrion crow, magpie).

The seed and berry eaters have come from the north and east of Europe. The redwing, field-fare, brambling and siskin are almost always found in flocks, roaming around in search of good feeding sites. Their food is usually found concentrated in large quantities in particular places. This means that they do not get in one another's way, and joining other members of the

same species also has the great advantage of enabling them to benefit from one another's information about sources of food.

The insect eaters' food, in contrast, is very widely dispersed. This is why you will seldom see robins, wrens and blackbirds operating in flocks. By remaining on their own, they each have a better chance of scraping enough food together to survive.

A lot of wrens die of starvation in hard winters, but by raising an extra large number of young in the next few seasons, the survivors are able to repair the damage within a couple of years. However, the rule that insect eaters live individually does not always apply. In winter, tits, goldcrests and treecreepers fly through the woods in mixed flocks.

In this case it is also food that brings them together. The small insects and insect eggs they rely on are hidden in crevices and splits and are not that easy to find. This means it is worth while seeing what other individuals have found. These flocks are not particularly close-knit. The members change all the time, and as soon as the need for it disappears, the flock will cease to exist.

Invaders

The invaders are a special category of winter visitors. These are species that you do not see every winter, but in some years they suddenly arrive in huge numbers. This sort of invasion is the result of a shortage of food, which has forced the birds to leave their breeding grounds where they would normally remain. This phenomenon occurs mainly in birds that eat the fruit of trees and bushes. Many trees and bushes bear a glut of fruit one year, and almost nothing the next. In glut years the birds rear large numbers of young; the following year there is not enough for all these birds to eat and they set out in search of better feeding grounds. Perhaps Britain's best-known and most striking invaders are the waxwings, while Western Europe is also frequently invaded by the nutcracker. Waxwings breed in the coniferous forests of Northern Scandinavia and Siberia. They live on berries in the winter, and as long as there are enough in the north there is no problem. But when food is scarce the waxwings leave in great flocks and appear anywhere there are berries, even in large cities. The nutcracker is a member of the crow family that eats predominantly conifer seeds. Occasionally Western Europe is swamped by nutcrackers from Siberia. They are normally permanent residents there, but in years when seeds are in short supply they move out en masse. It is easy to tell when one of these invasions is happening because nutcrackers are anything but shy and will allow people to approach very close.

The true nomads of the bird world are the crossbills, which specialize in feeding on fir and pine cones. The exceptional shape of their bill, with crossed mandibles, enables crossbills to extract the seeds from the cones. Unfortunately, conifers have the annoying habit of producing huge quantities of seed one year, and very little the next. So crossbills lead a wandering existence; they can be absent from an area for years on end, and then suddenly turn up again in great numbers. In prolonged periods of icy weather, more birds are forced to enter man's environment. It is the only place where they can still find food when supplies become scarce or inaccessible elsewhere. Then even fieldfares, redwings and bramblings overcome their natural shyness and appear in gardens.

The first signs of spring have scarcely appeared before the chaffinches, song thrushes and skylarks start back for their breeding sites. The first permanent residents occupy their territories. A new breeding season has begun.

Western Europe is occasionally overrun by nutcrackers from Siberia. These birds are usually permanent residents there, living on conifer seeds. In years when seeds are scarce they move out en masse. An invasion like this is easy to spot, because nutcrackers are anything but shy and will let you get really close to them

If it freezes hard, fieldfares will venture into gardens in search of food

CHAPTER 6

Songbirds and people

Songbirds are always admired. The song of the nightingale, lark and golden oriole has inspired composers, singers and poets down through the ages. In sharp contrast, however, many millions of songbirds are trapped or shot – in the past almost everywhere, now primarily in southern countries. In this country, most people are more than willing to help and protect the songbirds in their own neighbourhoods. There are many ways of doing this.

Even more important than putting up nest boxes and feeding the birds in the winter is the way we shape our surroundings – specifically our gardens.

The species that are really having problems and whose continued existence is threatened cannot be helped in this way, because most of them are to be found in the countryside on the continent of Europe. The unprecedented scaling-up and intensification of agriculture is far and away the principal cause of the decline in the numbers of these birds. The only thing that can save them is a balanced agricultural and conservation policy.

Blue tit on a feeder. It is a good idea to feed the birds in periods of frost and snow. If the weather is not cold there is no need to feed them. In the breeding season it can even be harmful

The red-throated pipit nests on the tundra in the extreme north of Europe and spends the winter in North Africa and the Middle East

Hunting

In the countries around the Mediterranean tens of millions of songbirds are shot or captured every year. Sometimes they end up on the table, sometimes in a cage and sometimes they are used as decoys. The great majority, however, are simply used as targets, for 'sport'.

Northern Europeans generally condemn this wholesale slaughter. They are perhaps inclined to forget that in their regions it was not so long ago that great numbers of songbirds were captured and doomed to spend the rest of their lives languishing in a cage or aviary.

Finches, like the chaffinch, linnet, siskin, goldfinch and bullfinch, have traditionally been popular victims. 'Siskin limers' lured siskins on to twigs smeared with birdlime so that the birds could not fly away.

Along the Dutch coast, there were 'finchers' catching chaffinches on special 'finch runs', using decoy birds and fowling nets. Chaffinch singing competitions were popular in the south of the Netherlands and in Belgium. Large numbers of chaffinches were put into long rows of cages so that they could hear, but not see, one another.

The idea was that they would get into 'singing duels', until they were completely exhausted. The winner was the finch that could sing the most songs in a given time. Until recently chaffinches were often blinded with red-hot knitting needles because it was thought that this made them sing better.

There is still a lively trade in wild songbirds, even though it is illegal. Popular native aviary birds like the siskin, goldfinch and bullfinch may be kept, but they may no longer be caught. They must have a ring showing that they were bred in captivity.

Protection

Happily, our dealings with songbirds are generally a lot friendlier nowadays. Most of us like to see wild songbirds in our gardens and are very willing to do something for them.

There are many ways to make our own environment attractive to songbirds. While it is true that these are not species threatened with extinction, it is well worth while protecting the 'ordinary' birds close to home.

You can put up nest boxes in order to provide more species of birds with a nest site. It also means you can enjoy watching the birds at close quarters. Obviously nest boxes only benefit a small part of the bird population – the hole-nesters. They are useful where natural breeding sites –older trees with splits and holes– are in short supply, as is the case in many gardens. In a more natural environment it is better not to use nest boxes. Nest sites are seldom a problem here; and nest boxes also tend to mean that certain species are artificially encouraged at the expense of other species which are in fact more at home in that location.

Artificial nest sites are useful for species which are in danger of disappearing from a particular area as a result of a lack of suitable nest sites. This applies, for example, to starlings and house sparrows, which cannot find suitable nest sites on many modern housing estates. There are special nest bricks and nest tiles for

The pied wagtail is one of the songbirds that has adapted to man. It is consequently a widespread and numerous species. It will use all sorts of man-made structures -ranging from bridges and sheds to rubbish tips- as a nest site

The siskin, goldfinch and bullfinch are popular native aviary birds. They may be kept, but they may no longer be caught. They have to be ringed to show that they were bred in captivity

these species. Swallows can also use a little help in finding a nest site, but that does not necessarily mean they need artificial nests (although these do exist). Swallows can be helped by leaving the door or window to a shed or barn permanently open. They nest inside, but they cannot get into modern barns, which are completely closed. House martins build their nests against the outside wall, under the eaves. Some householders dislike the birds' droppings and consequently remove the nests. However there is a better way to prevent any nuisance: simply nail a shelf up under the nests.

What is much more important than supplying substitute nests is to provide a suitable habitat where birds can find food all year round. Anyone who has a garden can make it an attractive place for birds, for example by designing a varied planting in which lower-growing plants, bushes, trees and grass are interspersed and by planting native trees and

The little bunting can be identified by its brown cheek patch and light eye ring. It breeds in the north of Siberia and is an occasional visitor to the rest of mainland Europe

The pied wheatear is found in the extreme east of Europe, to the north of the Caspian and Black Seas. It also nests on Bulgaria's Black Sea coast

Starlings in a frost-covered tree. Extreme weather conditions like this provide wonderful pictures but make life very hard for the birds

A finch on a peanut ball. Birds will eat almost anything and there are many different ways of feeding them

Following pages: In winter, blackbirds are very grateful for berries on garden plants

shrubs, like hawthorn, elder, rowan and alder. They guarantee plenty of insect life, and many of them also bear berries to provide a rich source of food in the late summer and autumn. Dense low bushes and hedges attract many songbirds.

Maintenance is equally important. A sterile, tidy garden with not a weed in sight and raked within an inch of its life has very little to offer birds. Birds far prefer a bit of untidiness. So do not spray every last weed and insect (in fact, it is better not to spray at all), and do not weed and hoe every last little intruder. Leave some fallen leaves and twigs -if you have room, make a heap of dead branches, the wrens and dunnocks will thank you for it- and do not remove all the old stalks at the end of the growing season.

The people responsible for parks, verges and other 'public' green spaces can improve the chances for songbirds in a similar way, by providing a mixed planting with indigenous species, by avoiding the use of chemicals, by leaving some plant litter about, and by not mowing and pruning too often - particularly not in the breeding season!

In winter, we can help songbirds by feeding them. However, we should only do this during severe winter weather, when the birds can really use some extra food because their normal food is scarce and difficult to get at. In milder conditions, feeding can actually be counter-productive. You should never feed birds during the breeding season, because the young are then fed inappropriate food which can ulti-mately kill them. You can feed birds virtually anything, provided it will not swell up in their stomachs, like uncooked rice. (You should also soak dry, stale bread briefly before you put it out.)

There are all sorts of bird tables and bird feeders you can buy, and they all work pretty well. Position the feeding station out of the full sun, wind and rain, and make sure it doesn't become a canteen for the local cats with the birds as the only item on the menu.

The common rosefinch is thriving. This originally Eastern European species is extending its range far to the west. It has conquered almost all of Scandinavia and has been breeding in Holland every year since 1987

There are still many places where we can enjoy the song of the skylark. But this could change within the foreseeable future because numbers are declining fast. The skylark cannot keep pace with the rapid changes in farming practices

There is not a trace of red on the female common rosefinch. It is simply a little drab brown bird

The swallow is a familiar sight all over Europe. But the species is having a hard time and numbers are declining

Unpaved country lanes with lush verges and flower-fringed fields are an increasingly rare sight. And as they disappear so do feeding and nesting sites for birds

Threats

The songbirds you might come across in gardens and parks are generally thriving. In most countries, the numbers of robins, black-caps, great tits and chaffinches, to name just a few, have if anything increased rather than decreased in recent decades. This is due, of course, to the fact that they have adapted to the human environment.

But there are also songbirds that are not doing well at all – even species that are threatened with extinction. In almost every case, this is the result of human intervention in their habitat to which they are unable to adapt. Birds that live in the open are particularly vulnerable. Their original habitats, such as plains, moors and natural grasslands, have largely disappeared. For most species this did not present a problem, because agricultural areas more than compens-ated. While farming continued along traditional lines they were able to manage very well there

or even breed in much greater numbers than they had ever been able to before. But over the last forty years, in particular, farming has changed almost out of all recognition. Wild-flower meadows and extensively grazed pastures have vanished. Fields splashed with the red of poppies and the blue of cornflowers have been all but consigned to the history books. Large, uniform, fertilized expanses, kept weed-free with pesticides and intensively worked with state-of-the-art machinery, have taken over. Many birds, including songbirds, cannot keep up with the rapid pace of the changes in farming practices. There are still many places where we can enjoy the song of the skylark. But this could change within the foreseeable future, because numbers are drop-ping fast all over Europe. The swallow, still a familiar sight in Britain and Europe, is also in decline everywhere.

Numbers of corn buntings, typical residents of agricultural areas, have fallen sharply in

The grubbing out of hedgerows and thickets is one reason for the decline of the red-backed shrike. Red-backed shrike -this one is a male- build their nests there. They find their food, mostly large insects, on farmland

Just a few decades ago the crested lark was a common sight on new housing estates being built in Holland. They have all gone now. Much more dramatic is the decline in open grassland and farmland, where the great majority of crested larks nest

An endangered species: the masked shrike. A rare bird found only in the extreme southeast of Europe (Bulgaria, Greece and Turkey) where its numbers are declining

Western Europe. The changes in farming –the disappearance of rough patches and verges, fewer weed seeds in the fields, the replacement of cereals by maize and the absence of stubble fields in winter- mean that there is less and less food for these birds. The grubbing out of hedges and thickets, which have outlived their purpose and simply get in the way of the machines working the land, has contributed to the rapid decline of the red-backed shrike, the ortolan bunting and others.

The greatest changes are now taking place in the south and east of Europe. Here, plains and marginal agricultural areas are being destroyed at a great rate -with millions in EU subsidies- to make way for commercial forests, intensive farming, roads and industry.

In Spain, their principal habitat, the crested lark, tawny pipit and other 'plains' birds are being hit hard. The most seriously endangered songbird is the aquatic warbler, which is found in sedge marshes and traditional water meadows in river valleys in Eastern Europe,

particularly in Poland. Its biotope is vanishing fast. The existence of the aquatic warbler is under very real threat since the species occurs nowhere else in the world apart from Poland and Russia.

As an individual you cannot do anything to help these species directly, unless you own or manage a large piece of land. But you can contribute to the protection they so desperately need by joining forces with other people – for instance by becoming a member of one of the organizations for nature conservation which acquire and manage sites, for birds and other fauna and flora, such as English Nature, or by joining the Royal Society for the Protection of Birds, which is involved in measures of all kinds to promote the welfare of birds.

Following pages: There are fewer and fewer real meadows

Crows and magpies

The members of the crow family are classified as songbirds. Some people may find this hard to accept, because they hate crows and magpies. People try to destroy them because they are thought to do damage. 'Their numbers are increasing all the time', and 'They eat all the eggs and the young songbirds', are frequent accusations. So in many places crows are shot or trapped, their nests are shot to pieces or the eggs are removed. But do songbirds really suffer that much from the depredations of crows and magpies?

To start with, in recent decades crow and magpie numbers have certainly increased dramatically in a number of countries, particularly in Western Europe. This should not come as any surprise, since they are omnivores and we have made things easy for them with our throwaway society. In any case, there are also countries where the numbers have not risen at all. It is also true that crows and magpies take eggs and young birds. While it may not be pleasant to see a magpie with a young blackbird in its beak, this really is not something to get angry about. Nature is always a matter of eat and be eaten. Great tits eat caterpillars, blackbirds eat worms, magpies and crows occasionally eat a young great tit or a blackbird's egg. This a fact of life that we have to accept, just as we accept the cheetah that catches an antelope.

It would be a different story if songbird numbers were declining as a result of attacks by crows and magpies. But are they? The bird population is closely monitored in countries like Britain, Holland and Germany. And what do we find? During the same period when crow and magpie populations increased, the blackbird, great tit and all those other parks and gardens birds that are allegedly their victims flourished. Most species increased in numbers,

The carrion crow, hated by many, is as numerous as it is thanks to man. Destroying them is not only unnecessary, it is pointless. The gap left by a dead crow will soon be filled by another one

and not one declined. Individual areas (woods, parks etc.) where the nesting birds are counted every year, show the same result: an increase in crows and magpies and at the same time a rise in the populations of most of the smaller songbirds too. The possible impact of crows and magpies has also been investigated by comparing the numbers of songbirds in areas where crows and magpies are numerous with areas containing similar species of songbirds but where there are few if any crows and magpies. There proved to be no difference. And lastly, there have been studies that looked not at the numbers of songbirds, but at their breeding success rate – in other words the number of young they ultimately reared. Here again, the presence of crows and magpies had no effect. Just as many young songbirds grew to maturity in areas where there were crows and magpies as in areas where there were none.

There is only one possible conclusion to be drawn: the accusations laid at the door of crows and magpies are not justified. They do not deserve to be attacked in the way that they are: songbirds are no better off as a result. Regrettably, prejudices are hard to get rid of. Even factual arguments cannot always eradicate them. Some people prefer to go by something they saw once with their own eyes, rather than the findings of research based on thousands of careful observations. But who knows, my words may change the convictions of a few crow-haters. Because there is no reason to treat crows and magpies differently from any other bird. They have just as much right to exist.

The jay is another member of the crow family that sometimes eats eggs and young birds, although these items form a very small part of its diet. Their activities have no effect whatsoever on songbird numbers

Some people assert that there are fewer songbirds because magpies eat them 'all'. The magpie -a songbird itself- eats anything, including the occasional egg and young bird. But research has shown that this has absolutely no effect on the numbers of the prey species. The songbird populations in parks and gardens, which allegedly suffer so badly from magpie depredations, are not declining at all - in fact they are increasing

Index of
Latin names

(the species marked with * are not mentioned in the main text, only in photographs and captions)

Index of common names

Photography credits and acknowledgements

L. Boon, Groningen: pp. 8 top left and top right, 10, 11 bottom, 14 right, 15 bottom right, 16, 17 right, 18, 20 top right and bottom, 22, 26, 27, 31 top left, 33 right, 35 right, 38 right, 42 left, 45, 46, 47 right, 49 top and bottom, 51, 52, 53 top right, 54, 58 top right, 58 bottom, 59, 60 top left, 61, 67, 68 right, 70, 71 bottom left, bottom right, 76 top, 79, 82, 83 top left, 90, 91, 92-93, 97 top, bottom left and bottom right, 98 bottom, 99 top right and bottom, 100 left, 101 bottom, 105, 107 centre left, bottom and right, 116 top left and right, 121 right, 122, 123 left, 126, 128, 129 left, 132 bottom left, 134 right, 135, 138.

J. Boshuizen, Amsterdam: pp. 53 top left, 87, 89, 94, 96 top.

J. van Holten, Schiedam: pp. 4, 6, 17 left, 31 bottom right, 32, 33 left, 39 right, 48, 83 top right, 95, 102, 106, 110-111.

H. Hut, Ten Boer: pp. 5, 8 centre, bottom and right, 11 top, 14 left, 15 top and bottom left, 19, 20 top left, 21, 23, 24-25, 28-29, 31 top right, 34, 35 left, 36, 37, 38 left, 39 left, 40-41, 43 right, 49 centre, 50, 53 bottom, 55, 56-57, 58 top left, 60 centre, bottom left and right, 62 right, 63 top left, 65, 66, 68 left, 69, 72-73, 74, 76 bottom, 77, 78, 80-81, 83 bottom, 85, 86, 88, 96 bottom, 97 centre, 98 top, 101 top, 103, 107 top left, 108, 109, 112, 113 right, 114, 115, 116 bottom left, 117, 118 left, 119, 120 left, 121 left, 123 right, 125, 127, 129 right, 130-131, 132 top left and right and bottom right, 133, 134 bottom left, 136-137, 139.

J. v.d. Leijgraaf, Huissen: pp. 12-13, 30, 31 bottom left, 62 left, 63 bottom left and right, 71 top right, 99 left, 100 right, 113 left, 118 right, 120 right.